BEFORE I LAY ME DOWN TO SLEEP

PROPHETESS TAMMY METCALF

© Copyright, 2016

By

Tammy Metcalf

ISBN – 978-0-692-7680-4-4

Library of Congress In-Publication-Data

Cover designed by DG Publishing

Tallahassee, Florida

Edited by Jacqueline Harper

DG Publishing Press
dgpublisingpress.com

Preface

At times I feel like I've lived three or four different lives. I feel that each life was a complete and different stage - and yet they were interlocking. They seem to be like a wooden fence that has separate stakes each one independent of itself and connected by one or two separate pieces of wood.

Every stage of my life has come with losses and with gains; it is from those losses and those gains that I acquire lessons learned. I gained some things and I have lost some things.

As I look back, I can see that whether gain or loss I have learned. I realize that all are needed to form growth, character and the person that I have become today and will be tomorrow.

One day I received a text from my youngest daughter which read, "If you had just one thing to tell me before you died, what would it be?" The text caught me off guard, but it also got me thinking of what *lessons I would want to teach before "I Lay Down to Sleep." As you read this book I pray that as you continue on your journey of life you will be inspired to reach for and seek to achieve the rewards of these lessons learned...*

Contents

1. Know God for Yourself And Establish Your Own Relationship

2. Find Your Own Voice

3. Don't Allow Others to Judge You or Set Your Standards

4. Believe That You Have a God-Given Ands Constitutional Right to Express Yourself

5. Love from the Inside Out

6. Find Your Worth in the World

7. Learn to Truly Forgive

8. Be Here Now

Knowing God for Yourself

Lesson 1 - Knowing God for Yourself

Seek and Ye Shall Find... It seems that with all the distractions in our lives today one of the things we forget is building our own relationship with God. It has become so easy to get a quick fix by just going to church or listening to a few songs over the radio that stir the emotions, or it may be a heart wrenching message. These days anyone can turn on the television and get a whole church service and never have to get out of his/her pajamas. Don't get me wrong. I have nothing against church

1

or Christian television. I strongly support both but too often we fail to realize the purpose behind all of the preaching and teaching. The purpose behind the message and the music is to introduce and inspire you to seek God yourself.

You may be saying to yourself, but I get what I need at church. I feel good when I leave. Well praise God. You should but there is more. God wants you to get to know him personally. Hearing about Him through the preacher is wonderful but God wants to share His secrets with you. Before Gary, my husband, and I began dating I knew of him, and I knew somethings about him. Most of the things I heard about him came from someone other than him. It wasn't until we started dating and spending time together that I got to know him, and in knowing him, I found out much more about him than anyone had ever told me.

Our Father in Heaven wants you to get to know more about him than anyone could ever tell you. In John 15:15 NIV Jesus is having a conversation with

His disciples and He tells them, "I no longer call you servant, because a servant does not know his master's business, instead I have called you friends for everything that I have learned from my father I have made known to you." The only way he was able to make it known to them was to spend time with them and share intimate time with them.

This is what the Father wants to do for you. He longs to spend intimate time with each of us. He doesn't want you to only get word - of - mouth knowledge about Him. He wants to call you friend he wants you to know His plans for your life. He wants you to know Him personally. How do we get to know God for ourselves? I would love to say that that is, simple, but that is not always the case. Life is busy and it doesn't slow down for us, but we must be intentional about slowing our lives down enough to read scripture, to pray (talk to God) and then to hear from God. I know you say I read the Bible and I pray, but do you stop and wait to hear what He has to say to you? You see friends have conversations. That means one person talks and the other listens then responds. That's what God wants to do with us. Yes, it may take some getting used to but it will be well worth it. It will change your life so begin today. Slow down from your weekly hectic routine and read a few scriptures and talk to God. If you've never talked to Him before, then it might feel a little uncomfortable at first. But the more you do it and the more you read the easier it will get. You may be asking, how do I seek God if I can't see Him? That is what faith is all about - the substance of things not seen and the evidence of things hoped for.

The Reward of Seeking God... It is okay to ask God who He is because he has answered it, "I am Alpha and Omega... The beginning and the end." He is a comforter, a guide, a healer, a friend, a mother, and a father. If you have any questions about God take them to Him and He will answer them. The bible says, 'My sheep know my voice and will not follow another." That means if you listen He will speak to you and you won't be lead down the wrong path by another voice.

If you are wondering how God speaks or what His voice sounds, like maybe it sounds like a human or a bird or maybe a thunderbolt. The answer is none of these. God speaks to our heart and mind. Have you ever had a gut feeling about something or said, "Something told me to do that?" Well, that feeling was the Spirit of God and it will guide you if you listen and learn to be obedient. Just as a child knows his or her mother's or father's voice by hearing it daily, you will begin to know your Father's voice when you spend time with Him daily.

Finding a Voice

Lesson 2 - Finding a Voice

We are the product of our surroundings. This includes family who imparted the do's and don'ts into our lives, the people we call our heroes whether it be because they look good, their behavior is one that we admire or because we deem them as a trusting and reliable source, such as our pastor, policemen, or teacher. We are also a product of some negative events that have either positioned us in a corner to change our views or has given us the power to be vengeful. The acquisition of circumstances and situations (present and past), surroundings, heroes, enemies, learned facts, education, and plain old lessons learned are the core of our belief systems. All of this will help you to understand why people have so many different opinions about something that may seem just plain black or white to you. No two people have had the same circumstances or situations. Two people may have the same life experience and come out with two different life lesson. You see a lesson has very little to do with the experience you have; it has more to do with the way you view the experience.

If you are to find your voice, and by that I mean speak from the viewpoint of your own experiences without fear of being criticized for not going along with the status quo, you must embrace the things that you believe in and not change them simply because someone else does not agree. Your voice comes from what you believe in and for what you stand.

Take time and do an inventory on yourself. Ask yourself questions like, "How do I feel about the path in life I am taking? Am I even taking a path or am I just playing follow the leader?" What do I expect to gain from this path? Does this path line up with the path God has for me? Whatever your answers are ask yourself, "Why do I believe this is a good or bad path for me?"

Why do you believe what you do?

The Civil War was fought on American soil, and all parties involved in the fight were Americans. But Approximately 625,000 men died in the Civil War that is more deaths than WW1, WW2, the Korean War and the Vietnam War combined.

So what I am saying is more than 625,000 men from the same country with the same allegiance to the same country had two different beliefs about the value of human life as it relates to skin color, and those two beliefs were so strong that they were willing to take up arms and place lives at risk so that their voice could be heard

You see whether right or wrong there will come a time in your life when you will have to defend what you believe. My question to you today is. Is what you believe worth standing up for? Is it worth fighting for? Jesus said, "Whosoever will lose his life for my sake shall find it" (Matthew 16:25 DRA).

Rewards of finding your own voice... Finding your own voice can give you endurance power. It gives you the purpose behind your passion and you will be less likely to be tossed here and there like the wind. Once God's voice is heard your life will become fueled by passion and purpose.

Don't Allow Others to Judge or Set Your Standard

Lesson 3 - Don't Allow Others to Judge or Set Your Standards

As you walk this journey called life, you will encounter many people with oh so many opinions and so much advice. Many of these people are well meaning, but others are either jealous or just opinionated.

In one of the previous lessons I mentioned where people get their belief system. Finding two people who have walked the same path in life would be almost impossible. That's why people have so many viewpoints on one topic.

Have you ever had a conversation with someone and whatever subject you talk about they find a similar one that happened in their life and tell you how they handled it emphasizing the different way they handled it? Only you have walked your path and only God knows all of your encounters as those who tried to belittle or judge you. There is only one Judge and He judges us all.

If you have a dream or a goal, don't let anyone tell you it can't be achieved. No one can measure how much determination you have. Only God knows what He has placed inside of you.

Secondly, don't allow people to tell you it has never been done like that or we do it like this. If you find a better way of doing something, don't be afraid to try it. If no one ever tried anything different there would be no innovative ways of doing things. We would still be riding horses and carriages, we'd have no electricity. Don't be afraid to break down the barriers and change the norm.

Rewards of setting your own standards... Bill Gates was a college dropout, and he invented a computer operating program that made him a millionaire, not the standard way of doing things.

If you don't allow yourself to be caught up in what others think about you, you will have more time to spend doing things you want to do. God created you in His image. All the gifts inside of you he placed them there; therefore, allow others to tell you that you are limited in your abilities, skills, dreams or goals. You can do all things through Christ because He is the One who strengthens you. Be like the eagle. Rise above the judgment, and set your own standards. Just see how far you will soar.

You Have a Right to Your Desires, Wants and Needs

Lesson 4 - You Have a Right to Your Desires, Wants and Needs

When God created Adam, he had already prepared all his wants and needs. There was a place for him to live, food to eat, water to drink, air to breathe and beauty to look at. Then He formed Eve to meet Adam's desires and to be a soulmate. You must understand that God created you and knows everything about you; if He prepared for Adam, surely He will not deny you.

You have a God - given right to your desires and wants as long as they do not impose on the rights of others. For

17

Instance, God does not mind if you want a red BMW if you are willing to work and pay for it. He doesn't mind if you want your neighbor's red BMW, but if you plan to steal it, then you are imposing on his right to maintain his property and he might defend his property by his right to bear arms. Do not feel guilty if you have strong desires as long as they are not ungodly; don't let others talk you out of it. You have a right.

Rewards- Accepting that there's nothing wrong with you because your desires, wants, and needs are different from others' as long as it's not contrary to the Word of God will give you the freedom to nurture the possibilities and the room to focus and make plans to acquire these desires, wants, and needs. Just remember not at others' expense or if they are out of the will of God. Don't give up your wants, desires, or needs because others believe it is their right to tell you how wrong you are.

Love Yourself from the Inside Out

Lesson 5 - Love Yourself from the Inside Out

Have you ever been asked to tell or write something about yourself and find out that you don't know what to say or you can only talk about what you have or your children? If I asked you to tell me something about your brother or sister, you would probably think of a whole lot of things to say.

That's because we spend more time finding out about other people than ourselves. If you were to ask a chef for the ingredients in a delicious cake he made, you wouldn't want to hear about the store he brought the ingredients from or the chicken or the vegetables before the dessert; you would want to know what was in the cake. Same with you and me. We talk about surface things like hair, nails, clothes, and belongings; but, in order to love ourselves inside out first we must spend some quiet time with our self and discover what we like. Are we patient or impatient?

Here's an example. If you were a teacher, and I asked you why you wanted to become a teacher would you say because I like to teach or could you know yourself well enough to know that you have a thirst and a passion to learn and a desire to share what you have learned with others.

The Bible teaches that every good and perfect thing comes from above (the Father). Now if that is true, once you have searched yourself and accepted the good qualities and traits God has placed in you, you will begin loving you - what's in you from the inside. You will realize that the outside is quite superficial to the beauty on the inside.

Have you ever tried to force a smile when you were mad or angry? Not a very pretty smile, is it? Now compare it to when you are happy or something is funny. It is a very different smile, isn't it. What I'm saying is what's on the inside will be expressed on the outside.

It doesn't matter how beautiful you are on the outside. If you have a bad attitude, low self-esteem, it will be conveyed in your outer appearance. Have you ever seen an unattractive person with a lot of friends? It's as if people just flock to them.

That person has learned to accept and acknowledge something about himself/herself whether it is their humor, compassion or friendliness. I do not believe beauty is only skin deep, I believe physical beauty is skin deep, but true beauty begins in the heart.

Rewards- Loving yourself from the inside out... Once you have acknowledged, accepted, and learned to love the good qualities and traits God has placed in you then you will be less likely to allow people to intimidate you, hurt your feelings, or enlist you, to change to their requirements. You will then have an understanding that God made you, and He gave you all those wonderful gifts inside of you. Then you will begin to love and cherish the God in you.

Find Your Worth in the World

Lesson 6 - Find Your Worth in the World

On just about any day, in any state, in any city, on any street, or in any house you'll find someone who will say he or she is looking for love. But what are they truly searching for? Psychologists suggest that as far as love goes, people give out their need, which should mean that I give love because I need love. Unfortunately, that's not always true. What we give is sex, lust and lies expecting love in return.

Too many young people have been left to figure out what love is for themselves. Due to a decline in social and family structure; television and magazines have accepted the challenge to explain to your youth what love is. But the sad thing is that their explanation is faulty and leads them from one broken heart to another or one relationship to another. Let's explore what T.V. and magazines say love is...

Sex- T.V. gives illustrations on daytime and night time drama. It makes fornication and adultery the in thing to do.

Lust- It's sexy to dress provocatively so people will lust after you. It's okay if you lust, and we'll show you how to get it.

Lies- Deception never reveals your heart to the games people play.

Now what does God say about these three?

Sex- To be shared by a man and a woman after marriage; the marriage bed is undefiled

Lust- If you lust after women, you have already committed the sin.

Lies- Satan is the father of lies.

Look at the difference in what God says love is and what the world says love is. It's no wonder so many of us are looking for fool's love just like fool's gold. It's pretty at first, but very soon it will tarnish because it was never real. So you ask, How will I know what love is when I find it?"

1. You will never find it if you don't make preparation to receive it. This will include loving yourself from the inside out as talked about in the previous chapter.
2. Forgiving (which we will talk about in a later chapter.)
3. Stop giving fool's gold.

The Bible says:

* God made man in His image and He said it was good and He loved man and he gave him dominion.
* God so loved the world that He gave His only begotten son.

- Submit yourself one unto the other in love and humility.
- Husbands love your wives as Christ also loved the Church.

Considering the above script let us translate what love does according to God. In script 1 and 2 God gave something because He loved, He didn't give money, diamonds or cars. He anticipated the desire or the need and gave out of sacrifice and compassion: Let's go a little deeper, God created Adam in His image so he knew Adam had abilities and qualities and would have the desire to have dominion so He gave him everything that He made. In the 2nd scripture God knew man would need a Savior, He had compassion on man and anticipation. Then, He gave something that was close to him, it was a sacrifice. So love is knowing or anticipating a need or desire given out of compassion even if it requires sacrifice. Love does not require the other person to be worthy or meet some financial qualification.

Reward- If you can learn that you do not have to offer sex to fulfill desires of lust or lies in order to receive love if you can learn that you are worthy of love just because God created you and if you will receive and allow God to express His love to you, then no longer will you be enticed to fool's love. You will never settle for less than you deserve, and you will not sell yourself short because you will realize how much you are worth to this world and to God.

Learn to Truly Forgive

Lesson 7 Learn to Truly Forgive

The Bible teaches that we should forgive those who sin against us as He (the Father forgives us). For years I believed that if I spoke the words I "forgive you" then I had forgiven, but instead I was just pressing it further down in my heart. If you look at the news today, you see reports of innocent children being raped, kidnapped, and molested - many in their own homes.

How did we get here and how do we stop breeding this type of behavior? I believe it all starts with forgiveness not only forgiving the perpetrator, but forgiving the ones you might consider responsible for your safety as well as forgiving yourself for either remaining silent or feeling like you could have done more. Un-forgiveness is like putting a piece of meat in a jar closing it and letting it sit for months. Eventually maggots will begin to form and eat away at the meat. That's what un-forgiveness does to our Heart. It eats away at any good thing, even to the point of self-destruction.

Have you ever heard someone say, "I can forgive you, but I can't forget?" in essence what they mean is I can forgive, but I chose not to. It's in the book of Micah 7:18-19 that we see God's character of mercy. Who is God like into thee that pardoned iniquity and passeth by the transgression of the remnant of his heritage? He retaineth not his anger forever, because he delighted *in* mercy. He will turn again, he will have compassion upon us; he will subdue our iniquities; and thou wilt cast all their sins into the depths of the sea. In this text the children of Israel have sinned against God but because of compassion and mercy God pardons them and does not remain angry with them. Micah goes as far as to say God throws the sin into a sea of forgetfulness. He says that because of God's mercy He will not give you what you deserve, and He will hold what you did over your head.

If God who is the creator of all things and can forgive and forget, then I do believe we should do the same. I am sure you are saying, "But how do I forget?" Unfortunately humans don't have an on and off switch for memory and that's okay. It's not the memory of the offense God is talking about. It's the hurt from the offense that he forgets. When I was about 10 years old, my brother and I were playing in the back yard where we had built a makeshift club house out of some old tin. In order to get inside you had to bend down real low, but one day I didn't bend down far enough, and a piece of tin sliced my right upper arm.

The slice was so quick and deep that I didn't even feel it; then a few minutes later I felt the warm blood running down my arm. It was only after I saw the blood that I ran to tell my mother what happened. After a few days of having my arm cleaned and bandaged up, the pain left. It took several weeks of having the wound covered for it to heal. Today 30 years later I still have that scar from that tin but I do not have pain from the scar.

Forgiveness is a God job. In our flesh we cannot and do not want to do it. If you will run to Jesus with the wounds of hurt, disappointment, and shame, He will clean your wounds, apply mercy and grace on them, and cover you until they are healed enough that they no longer cause you any pain. Once the pain is gone you may remember the place where the offense occurred, but you will no longer feel the pain.

Many times we acquire hurt and disappointment from people unnecessarily because we have unrealistic or unattainable goals for people that we have not even discussed with them. There is a saying that I feel is very true, "When people show you who they are, believe them". Sometimes we are hurt or disappointed because we have set our expectations of people too high. This is so common with women because God created us to be nurturers; He created us to be the ones to see the potential in everything. What happens is that although you may see and want the best for that person, that person may not be assigned to you. They may not be ready so when they don't meet your expectations of them, you get broken hearted and feel like you were betrayed or let down. Jesus said that with His strips we are healed. He is not just talking about the physical; He's also talking about emotional and spiritual wounds. I would be lying to you if I said forgiving is easy, but I will say that with Christ all things are possible and easier than without him. *Rewards:* If you will allow God to help you forgive and let go of what you feel others deserve for hurting or disappointing you, you will open up doors for God to forgive you and not give you what He feels you deserve for hurting Him. Forgiving releases you to grow in God's love and grace.

Be Here Now

Lesson 8 Be Here Now

I have often found myself physically in the middle of doing something while mentally in the middle of doing something else. This is not a good way to have the best life. I have always been a multi-thinker tasker. This means that most time while I am doing one thing, I am either doing something else or thinking about another thing. Mental business is a thief, which steals moments that you will never get back. It steals the best conversations and memories from you.   "Be here now" is a phrase that I constantly tell myself in order to bring my mind into focus. Being in the moment of life will enable you to feel life, to smell flowers, to see the smiles on your children's or grandchildren's faces. So many times we miss the beauty of our lives because we are living it out in our heads. Mentally we are thinking about the next thing we have to do or the last thing we did. Our lives can seem so cluttered and we get overwhelmed when we live life in our brain.

One day I was talking to my husband and I was sharing with him the things I had done that day; midway through my list he said, "Babe, you have done a lot of stuff and you haven't even gotten out the bed yet." I wasn't lying to my husband I had been sorting out the details of my day in my head long before I even stepped out of bed. This was not bad, but it was tiring.

I even had a solution for when things that I planned in my head didn't go as planned. I had a plan A, B, and even C. This all sounds nice, but it's tiresome and mentally draining. While you are planning to live, you are missing out on living. I'm not saying don't make plans, but don't' miss out on what's in front of your planning ahead in the future.

Put your trust in God and believe that He is able to carry you through whatever the day brings. As I look back on life I realize that I spent too much daily time running around responding to situations that either did not go as I had planned or I had not planned for it at all.

A few years ago I was lying in a hospital bed very close to death. My only concern at that time was if I had done everything I was assigned in this life to do. God doesn't want us giving Him excuses as to why we didn't do our assignment while we were alive. I don't want to stand before a God who has made all the resources available for us to carry out His plan for our lives and say I didn't have time.

I would imagine his answer would be: you did not use your time wisely. You can never regain time, once it's gone that's it. Don't waste it by being mentally busy and physically in the wrong place at the wrong time. Do not try to be the master of your own fate; allow God to be in control of your life. Just follow his lead. The Father cares for you and knows what is good for you. Listen to that quiet still voice and let Him take you where His plan leads. We are not the makers of this life nor the makers of ourselves or others. We have simply no idea how intertwined our lives are with others. But God knows all and sees all and is able to handle it all. If we let God do His job, then we could truly enjoy this life He has given us.

Reward: Be here now, make every moment of your life precious and important. It allows you the opportunity to see the beauty in yourself and others around you.